# KINGS ✤ AND ✤ QUEENS

# Henry VIII

*Katrina Siliprandi*

## Wayland

Titles in the series

# Elizabeth I
# Henry VIII
# James VI/I
# Mary Queen of Scots
# Queen Victoria
# William I

**Series editor:** Sarah Doughty
**Book editor:** Margot Richardson
**Consultant:** Mark Dartford
**Designer:** Jean Wheeler
**Picture researcher:** Liz Moore
**Production controller:** Carol Stevens

First published in 1995 by Wayland (Publishers) Ltd
61 Western Road, Hove, East Sussex, BN3 1JD, England

**British Library Cataloguing in Publication Data**
Siliprandi, Katrina
Henry VIII – (Kings & Queens series)
I. Title  II. Series
941.

ISBN 0 7502 1448 1

Typeset by Jean Wheeler
Printed and bound in Italy by Rotolito Lombarda S.p.A.

**Picture acknowledgements**
The Bodleian Library 17 (bottom); The Bridgeman Art Library 5 (left, Fitzwilliam Museum, University of Cambridge), 8, 15 (bottom), 21 (bottom), 23 (top); The British Library 11 (top), 16; The College of Arms 10, 12 (bottom); E.T Archive 4 (Pepys Library, Magdalen College, Cambridge), 9 (bottom, by courtesy of Her Majesty the Queen), 12 (top, Trustees of the British Museum); Mary Evans 5 (right); Fotoatelier Gerhard Howald 22 (top); Fotomas Index 13 (bottom); Historic Royal Palaces (Crown Copyright) 21 (top), 27 (top); Jarrold Publishing 19 (top); Magdalen College, Oxford 6 (top); The Mansell Collection 13 (top), 15 (top), 18, 20, 22–3 (bottom),  29 top; National Portrait Gallery 7, 14 (top), 17 (top), 25 (top), 26, 27 (bottom); Norfolk Air Photographs Library (Derek A Edwards) 24; Public Record Office 29 (bottom); Royal Armouries 28; The Royal Collection © 1994 Her Majesty The Queen 6 (bottom), 25 (bottom); The President and Fellows of St. John's College, Oxford 26; Skyscan Balloon Photography 14 (bottom); Victoria and Albert Museum, courtesy of the Trustees of the V&A/P Barnard 11 (bottom); by courtesy of the Dean and Chapter of Westminster 9 (top).

# Contents

# Henry Becomes King

*A page from the 'Anthony Roll' of 1546, showing the* Mary Rose. *The roll was a list of all Henry VIII's ships and their equipment. The roll was published one year after the sinking of the* Mary Rose.

On 19 July, 1545, the *Mary Rose*, a warship, sank near Portsmouth on the south coast of England. Henry VIII, the King of England, watched with horror from the shore. The *Mary Rose* was one of about sixty ships, preparing to do battle with the French. It had holes in its sides for its giant guns, and was probably trying to sail with these uncovered. Water rushed through the holes into the lower deck, causing the *Mary Rose* to capsize. Almost all the crew of 500 men 'drowned like ratten' [rats].

*(Above) An artist's impression of how Henry looked as a child.*

*(Left) Henry, aged about thirty-six. When he was young people said he was the most handsome prince in Europe.*

By that date, 1545, Henry VIII had been king for thirty-six years. Many changes had taken place during this time. He had married six women. All the monasteries had been closed down. At the start of his reign Henry had been very rich, but now he was almost bankrupt. He had been handsome, but now he was enormously fat with painful legs.

Henry was born on 28 June, 1491, in the royal palace at Greenwich in Kent, 8 km south-east of London. His mother was Elizabeth of York, his father was the first Tudor king, Henry VII. He grew up with his mother, his older brother Arthur and his sisters, Margaret and Mary. Most of his childhood was spent at the royal palaces near London: Greenwich, Eltham and the palace of Sheen, later renamed Richmond.

## IMPORTANT DATES

**1491** *Henry VIII born.*

**1501** *Henry VIII's brother, Arthur, marries Catherine of Aragon.*

**1502** *Arthur dies.*

**1509** *Henry VII dies. Henry VIII marries Catherine of Aragon. Henry VIII crowned King of England.*

*A treaty was made in 1488, agreeing that Catherine of Aragon should marry Arthur. Arthur was only two years old at the time. This tapestry, made later, shows their **betrothal**.*

Henry was given an excellent education. He learned to speak and write four languages. He also learned how to behave on public occasions. Desiderius Erasmus, a Dutch scholar, said that as a child Henry had 'a vivid and active mind, above measure able to execute whatever tasks he undertook'. From an early age he had some state duties to perform, but not as many as his brother Arthur who was expected to become king.

Arthur married Catherine of Aragon, the daughter of the king and queen of Spain, when he was fifteen years old. But only five months later Arthur died. Henry became Prince of Wales, but he took no part in governing England. He spent his time riding, hunting, **hawking** and **jousting**. He greatly enjoyed wrestling and was a good **archer**.

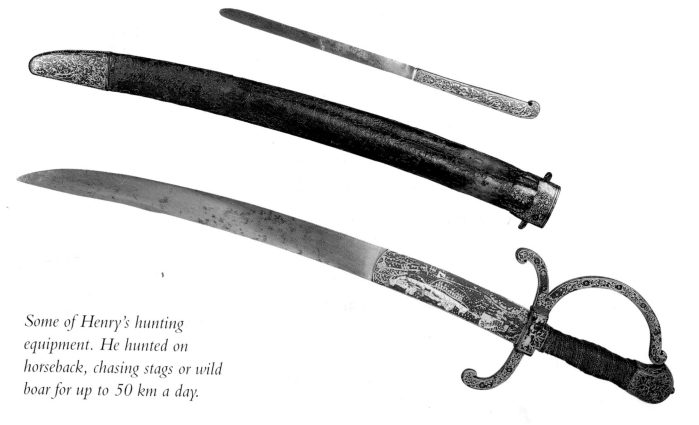

*Some of Henry's hunting equipment. He hunted on horseback, chasing stags or wild boar for up to 50 km a day.*

*Henry dressed very carefully to show off his wealth and power. The Venetian ambassador wrote 'his robes are the richest and most superb that can be imagined'.*

In 1509, Henry's father, Henry VII, died. The young Henry became king, aged seventeen. At first he was very popular. Thomas More, a lawyer and scholar, wrote that Henry was 'the greatest, the best, and to use a new and very honourable title for a king, the most loved'. Henry was tall with broad shoulders, fair skin and long, red-gold hair. His voice was high pitched. An **ambassador** from Venice, called Pasqualigo, wrote that he had 'a round face, so very beautiful that it would become [suit] a pretty woman, his throat being rather long and thick'.

*Catherine of Aragon, Henry's first wife. They were married for more than twenty years.*

Henry married his brother's widow, Catherine of Aragon, and they remained married for much of his reign. She was an attractive woman, with grey eyes and long golden-brown hair.

Henry wrote a poem to her:

As the holly groweth green,
and never changeth hue,
so I am, ever hath been,
unto my lady true.

Henry and Catherine rode in a procession through London on 23 June, 1509, the day before Henry was crowned as king. The crowds cheered enthusiastically. Henry was dressed in crimson velvet and a gold coat decorated with diamonds, rubies and emeralds. This showed his great wealth and power.

After his coronation, a **tournament** was held. People were entertained by jousting on horses and fighting on foot. Both the men and horses wore armour. In Tudor times, tournaments were held to honour foreign ambassadors, and also to celebrate holy days, treaties, royal marriages and births.

As soon as he became king, Henry released many prisoners. But some of the previous king's **ministers** were arrested. Two of them, Sir Richard Empson and Edmund Dudley, were beheaded. This made Henry very popular because many English people hated Empson and Dudley and blamed them for the **taxes** they had had to pay during the time of Henry VII.

*The coronation of Henry VIII at Westminster Abbey. After the coronation there was a great* **banquet***, followed by a tournament.*

*Henry wore clothes that were designed to make him look big and majestic. Here, shown with some of his family, he is wearing a padded jacket and cloak.*

# How Henry VIII Ruled

When Henry VIII became king he was very rich. He spent vast amounts of money on banquets and entertainments. At first he did not take part in tournaments because they could be dangerous. But in 1510, on the twelfth day after Christmas, Henry jousted in disguise. He did well and then he was recognized, which made him very popular. After that, he often joined in.

*Henry returning from a joust, watched by Catherine of Aragon and her ladies at the back of the picture. At Greenwich, Henry built a gallery for the royal family and important foreign visitors to watch the jousting. It was furnished with rich tapestries and cushions.*

Henry went to mass each morning and then loved to go hunting for stags and boars. He came back for supper at which he ate and drank an enormous amount. Henry also enjoyed wrestling, bowls, tennis, hawking, archery and music. He played the recorder,

**virginals**, and composed music. He also had other interests, including the study of Christianity. In the evening he liked to relax by dancing, playing cards and gambling with dice. All this did not leave much time for ruling the country.

Much of the government of England was left to his ministers. Henry disliked writing, which he thought was 'tedious and painful'. He did not even like to read letters. They were usually read to him and sometimes he told his ministers what to reply. Although Henry did not spend much time dealing with state business, many people believe he always took the final decision about things.

*(Above) Henry probably composed this piece of music. As well as playing music and singing himself, he employed large numbers of musicians at court.*

## IMPORTANT DATES

*1513*  *England at war with France and Scotland.*

*1514*  *Henry VIII makes peace with France and Scotland.*

 *Mary, Henry's sister, marries Louis XII of France.*

*1515*  *Louis XII dies.*

 *Francis I becomes the king of France.*

*1516*  *Mary (later Queen Mary I) born.*

*1520*  *Henry meets Charles V in England.*

 *Henry meets Francis at the Field of the Cloth of Gold outside Calais.*

 *Henry meets Charles V at Calais.*

*Henry's decorated writing desk can be seen in the Victoria and Albert Museum in London. There was a study next to the king's bedroom in all the important palaces where Henry could deal with state business.*

*In this painting Henry is eating 'alone', but he is still surrounded by courtiers. Even in his private life Henry lived in grand style.*

*Fighting on foot like this took place at a tournament. Henry VIII's armour can be seen at the Royal Armouries in the Tower of London.*

In late summer, Henry always went on a progress. This meant he travelled around the country staying in the houses of different **noblemen**. Henry also left the royal palaces if there was plague, smallpox or **sweating sickness** nearby. Many people died from these diseases in Tudor times.

Henry VIII ruled England, Wales, part of Ireland and the area around Calais, now in France. Henry wanted to rule all of France and he looked for glory by fighting wars. He spent great amounts of money on the army and navy. Many new warships were built during his reign, including the *Great Harry*, launched in 1514. She was the biggest ship in the world, with a crew of 700 men and twenty-one bronze cannons.

In 1513, Henry led an army to France. Three weeks later another of his armies defeated the Scots at Flodden. The Scottish king, James IV, was killed in the fighting. But Henry never succeeded in gaining control of either France or Scotland.

*(Left) Henry VIII in parliament, 1515. When Henry was king most people believed that it was their duty to obey him because the king's law was God's law. Henry got support for his new laws by having them passed as Acts of Parliament.*

*(Below) During the war with France, Henry besieged Therouanne, a town in France. This shows how siege warfare took place during Henry's reign.*

*Thomas Wolsey was the son of a butcher, but he became the richest and most powerful man in England, apart from the king.*

In 1514, Henry made peace with the French king, Louis XII. As part of the peace terms Henry's sister, Mary, had to marry Louis XII. He was old and toothless. Mary did not want to marry him because she was in love with someone else, but she obeyed her brother. Only two months later Louis XII died. The new French king was Francis I. Francis was as talented and ambitious as Henry VIII. Henry saw Francis as a rival. A Venetian ambassador, Giustinian, wrote that, 'on hearing Francis I wore a beard, he allowed his own to grow'.

Henry's chief minister and **Lord Chancellor** from 1515 was Thomas Wolsey. He was an ambitious man and he became very important. He was made a **cardinal**, and in 1518 he became the most powerful church man in England. He also became extremely rich. He loved to show off his wealth. He built a huge palace for himself by the River Thames at Hampton Court. It had 1,000 rooms and 500 staff to run it.

*Most of the Tudor buildings that visitors can see at Hampton Court today were built for Wolsey. These included buildings especially for Henry, Catherine of Aragon and Princess Mary when they came to stay.*

(Above) Henry VIII and Francis I met at the Field of the Cloth of Gold, near the border between the two kings' lands. The meeting lasted for two weeks, and involved the 3,000 most important people from both England and France.

Henry VIII and Francis I were keen to meet, but Henry did not want to upset another important European ruler, the Holy Roman Emperor, Charles V. So Henry first met Charles V in May, 1520, at Dover. In June, Henry met Francis at Guisnes, near Calais. The kings became friends, but three years later they were at war again.

From this portrait of Francis I, you can see that he cared about his appearance as much as Henry.

Many Europeans, including most English people, belonged to the Catholic Church. It was headed by the Pope, who lived in Rome. Some Europeans were unhappy about this. They were called Protestants because they 'protested' against some of the Catholic teachings. A German, called Martin Luther, expressed these ideas in a book called *De Captivitate Babylonica*. Henry VIII read it and wrote a book called *Assertio Septem Sacramentorum*.

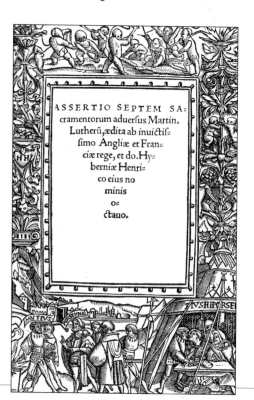

## IMPORTANT DATES

*1520*  Martin Luther's book published.

*1521*  Henry VIII's book published.

*1521*  The Pope makes Henry VIII Defender of the Faith.

*1523–6*  England at war with France.

*1528–9*  England at war with Charles V.

*1529*  Wolsey dismissed.

Thomas More made Lord Chancellor.

*1532*  More resigns.

*1533*  Cranmer becomes archbishop of Canterbury.

Henry VIII secretly marries Anne Boleyn.

Henry and Catherine's marriage judged unlawful by Cranmer.

Elizabeth (later Queen Elizabeth I) born.

*1534*  Act of Supremacy.

*1535*  More executed.

*1536*  Anne Boleyn executed.

Henry marries Jane Seymour.

*The title page from the book Henry wrote attacking the ideas of Martin Luther. In May 1521 Henry ordered that all Luther's books in England should be burned.*

This book condemned Luther. The Pope was pleased with Henry and gave him the title *Fidei Defensor*: Defender of the Faith.

By 1527, Catherine of Aragon was forty-two years old. She could not have any more children. Only one of her six children, Mary, had lived more than a few weeks. Henry still wanted a son to become king after him. He had also fallen in love with a young woman called Anne Boleyn, and wanted to marry her. He wrote her love letters: 'I would you were in mine arms or I in yours, for I think it is a long time since we kissed.'

Only the Pope could give permission to end Henry's marriage to Catherine. Henry ordered Wolsey to arrange this. It was known as 'the king's great matter'. The Pope refused. He did not want to upset Charles V, Catherine's nephew, who was against the divorce. Henry was furious. He blamed Wolsey, and in 1529, dismissed him, taking Hampton Court for himself. Thomas More was made the new Lord Chancellor.

*Anne Boleyn came to the English court in 1523. She soon attracted the king and they flirted openly.*

*Wolsey was arrested and sent to London for trial, but died on the way in a cold, stone room in Leicester. 'If I had served my God one half as well as I have served the king,' he said, 'He would not have left me to die in this place.'*

*The crown and the decrees shown here were signs of the Pope's power. This engraving shows what Henry and Archbishop Cranmer thought of the Pope.*

As the Pope would not allow his **divorce**, Henry took the English church from the Pope's control. He bullied the **clergy** into agreeing to this. They recognized him as the 'Supreme Head of the Church in England'. However, More was a loyal Catholic and he resigned. Thomas Cromwell, a solicitor who had worked for Wolsey, became Henry's leading minister.

Henry appointed Thomas Cranmer as Archbishop of Canterbury, because he knew Cranmer would give him a divorce. Cranmer declared that Henry and

Catherine's marriage was unlawful. By then Henry had already secretly married Anne because she was pregnant. Anne was crowned queen. Cranmer wrote that she was dressed 'in a robe of purple velvet, and all the ladies and gentlewomen in robes and gowns of scarlet'. Her baby was born on 7 September, 1533, and was named Elizabeth.

Henry decided that there should not be any mention of the Pope in the church prayer books. He ordered parish priests to cross out words about the Pope. Henry did not want to change the religious teachings of the church; he just wanted to get rid of the Pope as the head of the church. Henry remained against the ideas of Protestants, such as Luther.

*(Above) Anne Boleyn's bedhead. She took it with her from palace to palace during the progresses of the king and his court.*

*(Left) Thomas Cranmer was appointed Archbishop of Canterbury in 1533.*

Henry VIII decided that all English people should swear an oath that he was the supreme head of the English church. This was made law by the Act of Supremacy. Those who refused were beheaded, or hung, drawn and quartered. Thomas More would not take the oath and was executed. Many other people who supported the Pope were executed during Henry's reign, but so were many Protestants.

*Some of the people who disagreed with Henry VIII were executed by being burned.*

In 1536, Henry heard rumours that Anne Boleyn had other lovers. We do not know if these rumours were true. Maybe Henry decided he did not want her any more because she had not given him the son he wanted so much. Anne was imprisoned in the Tower of London. During the later years of Henry's reign the Tower was used less as a royal palace, and more as a prison. Whitehall became the usual place for the king to stay when he was in London. Some of Henry's prisoners were kept in harsh conditions and tortured, but most of them were treated quite well.

Anne spent the night before her execution in the same room she had used on the night before her coronation, less than three years before. The constable in charge of the Tower wrote that she said, 'I heard say the executioner was very good, and I have a little neck.'

Only ten days later Henry VIII married Lady Jane Seymour.

*This block and axe were used for beheadings at the Tower of London. Anne Boleyn was beheaded with a sword rather than an axe.*

*Jane Seymour was Henry's third wife.*

# Destruction of the Monasteries

*A monk as a wolf with a lamb in his mouth. It was meant to show that monks were greedy.*

Before Henry started changing the church there were about 600 **monasteries** in England. Between them, monks and nuns owned one-quarter of the fertile land. Thomas Cromwell and Henry VIII sent inspectors to each monastery, to check that the **monks** and nuns were living as they should. If the inspectors found that the monastery was not properly run it was closed down. This is what they found at Glastonbury: '... *found in his [the abbot's] study secretly laid a written book of arguments against the divorce of the king's majesty ... We have found a fair chalice of gold, and ... other parcels of plate, which the **abbot** had secretly hid.*'

## IMPORTANT DATES

*1535  Destruction of the monasteries begins.*

*1536  Rebellion begins.*

*1537  Edward (later King Edward VI) born.*

*Jane Seymour dies.*

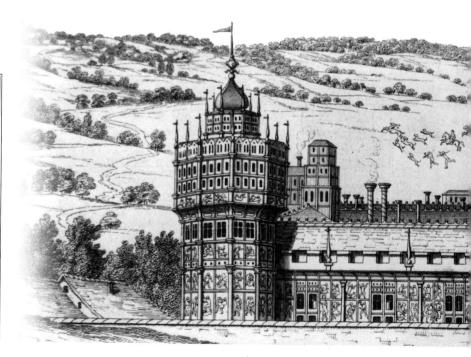

**Rebellion** broke out in parts of northern England. The rebels were angry about the destruction of the monasteries. They were also fed up with the high taxes they had to pay. They blamed Cromwell for these things. After the rebellion many of its leaders were hanged or beheaded. Corpses hanging on **gibbets** became a common sight in the north of England.

By now, Henry was having problems with his health. He was very fat, and had badly ulcerated legs. He could no longer joust, but still went hunting. He spent much time and money on building a new palace, called Nonsuch, in Surrey. It was meant to show how majestic he was.

*Thomas Cromwell led the destruction of the monasteries. Statues were smashed, books were burned, and stones were taken away to build houses for nobles and courtiers.*

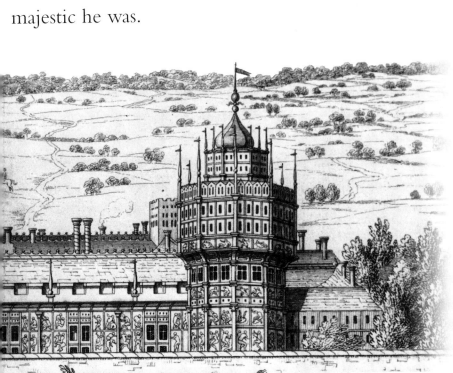

*Henry built Nonsuch Palace in the 1530s and 1540s. At his death he owned more than sixty houses, although only a few of them could house the whole royal court of over 1,000 people.*

*Castle Acre Priory in Norfolk was destroyed by Cromwell's men in 1539. From records that survive, historians know that about thirty monks lived there.*

Henry VIII and Cromwell continued to close down the monasteries. Abbots and **priors** were bribed with large pensions so that they voluntarily gave up their abbeys and priories. By the end of 1540, all of them were shut, and many of the buildings were destroyed. The king took over all the land, buildings and goods. During the rest of his reign he sold most of them, and used the money for more unsuccessful wars.

Henry and Cromwell also closed religious **shrines**. Henry thought they made people **superstitious**. The shrine at Canterbury, where St Thomas Becket was buried, was closed and his bones were removed. Henry took all the jewels and ornaments that pilgrims had given to the shrine.

In 1537, Queen Jane Seymour had a baby boy. Lord Chancellor Wriothesley wrote: 'at two of the clock in the morning the Queen was delivered of a man child at Hampton Court.' At last, Henry had a son. He was christened Edward.

A few days later Wriothesley wrote, 'Queen Jane departed this life, lying in childbed'. She died from blood poisoning. In Tudor times, medical knowledge was much less advanced, and having a baby was more dangerous than it is in Britain today.

*(Above) Henry's son, Edward. Although his birth and survival settled 'the King's Great Matter', Henry and Cromwell thought England could be made more powerful if Henry married the Duke of Cleves' daughter.*

*(Below) This portrait shows the king with Jane Seymour and Edward. On the left is Princess Mary, later Mary I, and on the right Princess Elizabeth, later Elizabeth I, although they could not have met at the ages they are shown here.*

# Henry's Last Years

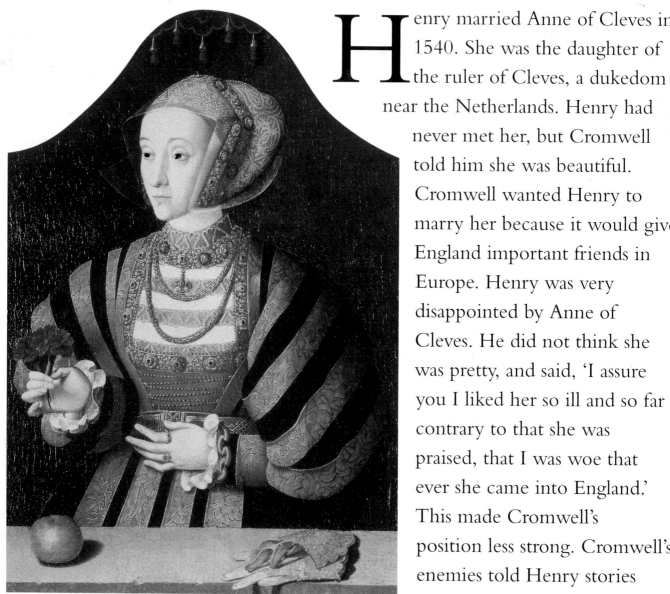

*Cromwell arranged for Henry to marry Anne of Cleves to make a link between England and Cleves, but Henry thought she was ugly.*

Henry married Anne of Cleves in 1540. She was the daughter of the ruler of Cleves, a dukedom near the Netherlands. Henry had never met her, but Cromwell told him she was beautiful. Cromwell wanted Henry to marry her because it would give England important friends in Europe. Henry was very disappointed by Anne of Cleves. He did not think she was pretty, and said, 'I assure you I liked her so ill and so far contrary to that she was praised, that I was woe that ever she came into England.' This made Cromwell's position less strong. Cromwell's enemies told Henry stories about him that were probably not true. Cromwell was arrested, charged with treason and beheaded.

Henry divorced Anne and married Katherine Howard. She was one of Anne's ladies-in-waiting, and was aged about nineteen. Henry had fallen in love with her. This marriage was a disaster. Henry was told that Katherine had had lovers before she was married. It proved likely that this was continuing after her marriage. Katherine was charged with treason and beheaded. One of her lovers was hung, drawn and quartered and another was beheaded.

Henry married once more. This time his choice was a good one: Katherine Parr looked after him and his three children until he died.

*(Above) A stained-glass window at Hampton Court, showing Henry and the family arms of his six wives.*

*(Left) Katherine Parr became Henry's last wife in 1543. She brought the three royal children to live together at court for the first time.*

KATHARINE PARRE

## IMPORTANT DATES

1540 *Henry marries Anne of Cleves.*

 *Henry divorces Anne of Cleves.*

 *Thomas Cromwell executed.*

 *Henry marries Katherine Howard.*

1542 *Katherine Howard executed.*

 *Henry declares war on Scotland.*

1543 *Henry marries Katherine Parr.*

 *Henry declares war on France.*

1545 *Mary Rose sinks.*

1546 *England and France make peace.*

1547 *Henry VIII dies.*

In 1543, Henry VIII and Charles V declared war on France. Henry was also fighting the Scots. His army attacked Edinburgh, and sent its people out of the city into the fields. The army spent two days burning the houses, but the castle was not captured.

Henry decided to lead the troops himself in France, and left Katherine in charge in England. By now he was extremely fat. We know from his armour that his chest measured 145 cm and his waist was 137 cm. He could hardly walk and had to be carried everywhere.

Henry sailed to Boulogne, in France, which the English army had captured. However, Charles V made peace with France without consulting Henry. Henry did not want England fighting France on its own so he returned home. The French tried, unsuccessfully, to invade England. This was when the *Mary Rose* sank.

*We know exactly what size Henry was from his armour. This set was made for him in 1540 in the royal workshops at Greenwich.*

Henry in about 1544. By now he was in pain all the time. He had breathing problems and an ulcerated leg that was possibly caused by a jousting injury.

(Below) The last page of Henry's will. In it, he said that the country should be ruled by a Regency Council until Edward was old enough to take power.

Henry and Francis I eventually signed a peace treaty, in 1546. The war had used up all Henry's money. He had to borrow money and raise taxes, and he also reduced the amount of gold and silver put in coins, so that he could keep it for himself.

A few months later, Henry died. He had been ill for a long time. For a Tudor he was an old man, as people usually died much younger than they do today. Henry VIII left a will that made his son, Edward, the next King of England.

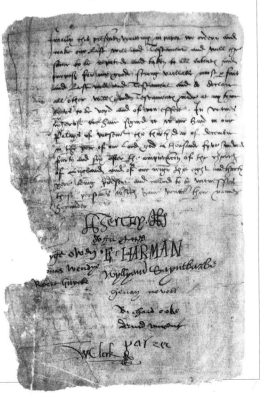

# Glossary

**abbot** A head monk, in charge of a group of monks in a monastery.

**ambassador** An official who represents his or her government in another country.

**archer** A person who uses a bow and arrows.

**banquet** A grand meal, with lots of food.

**betrothal** An agreement or promise for two people to marry each other.

**cardinal** Holder of the highest rank (after the Pope) in the Catholic Church.

**clergy** People who lead church services.

**divorce** The lawful end of a marriage.

**gibbet** A gallows, or metal cage, in which an executed body was put.

**hawking** Hunting by using hawks, or other birds of prey, to catch smaller animals or birds.

**Holy Roman Emperor** A name used by German kings to show their link with the Pope, and their importance in Europe

**jousting** Fighting between two knights on horses, with long spears, or lances.

**Lord Chancellor** One of the king or queen's most important advisors, responsible for the law courts.

**minister** A person given special government duties by the king or queen.

**monastery** Place where a group of monks live, work and worship.

**monk** A man following a religious life.

**nobleman** A rich and important man who had a title, such as a duke.

**nun** A woman following a religious life.

**pilgrim** A person who travels to a sacred or religious place in order to worship there.

**prior** An important monk, second in charge to an abbot.

**rebellion** An uprising against the people running the country, to try and replace them.

**shrine** A place with special meaning, or a tomb of a holy person or saint.

**superstitious** Believing in supernatural or mysterious things.

**sweating sickness** Disease of the lungs, probably influenza.

**taxes** Money that must be paid by people for the government and the services it provides.

**tournament** A fighting competition to entertain people.

**virginals** A keyboard instrument, like a piano.

# Further information

## Books to Read

### FOR CHILDREN

**Henry VIII** by Dorothy Turner (Wayland, 1994)
**Tudor Britain** by Tony Triggs (Wayland, 1989)
**Tudor Monarchs** by Jessica Saraga (Batsford, 1992)
**Tudors** by Donna Bailey (Headway, 1993)

### OTHER BOOKS OF INTEREST

**Henry VIII: Images of a Tudor King** by Christopher Lloyd (Phaidon, 1990)
**Henry VIII at Greenwich** by Margarette Lincoln, Barbara Reid and Leslie Rivett
  (National Maritime Museum, 1991)
**Life and Times of Henry VIII** by Robert Lacey (Weidenfeld and Nicolson, 1992)
**Mary Rose: Her Wreck and Rescue** by Ian Morrison (Lutterworth, 1988)
**Six Wives of Henry VIII** by Antonia Fraser (Mandarin, 1993)

## Places to Visit

**Castle Acre Priory, Castle Acre, King's Lynn, Norfolk**
A monastery that was closed by Henry VIII in about 1537.

**Hampton Court, East Molesey, Surrey**
The palace built by Cardinal Wolsey, and taken over by Henry VIII.

**Hever Castle, Edenbridge, Kent**
Anne Boleyn's childhood home. It is believed that Henry visited here while he was courting her.

**The *Mary Rose*, HM Naval Base, Portsmouth**
The remains of Henry's flagship, named after his sister, Mary Tudor.

**National Portrait Gallery, St Martin's Place, London, WC2**
Has some portraits of Henry VIII, his family and his parents, Henry VII and Elizabeth of York.

**Rievaulx Abbey, near Helmsley, North Yorkshire**
A twelfth-century abbey. Its walls still stand to their full height.

**Tintern Abbey, near Chepstow, Gwent**
A ruined abbey, where the church any many other buildings are still evident.

**HM Tower of London, London EC3**
Originally used as a royal palace, but later it was more often used as a prison.

# Index

Figures in **bold** refer to illustrations. Glossary entries are shown by the letter g.